The Call To Spiritual Sonship

By Julius H. Hummons

Table of Contents

DEDICATION

I dedicate this writing to first my wife Marietta. In the many years while this work was being birthed, she was the constant encouragement for seeing this work come to term. To my daughter and son, Jordan and Wesley who endured my times of being locked away in my office, I dedicate this work. Without the love and support of my family this writing would not have brought me to place of truth expressed in this work. My greatest thanks is to my Father God who designed, purposed and inspired me to know He is my true Father. By the Spirit of God and His Word I commit this writing to the body of Christ. There is nothing of me worth speaking without the inspiration and guidance of God my Father.

PREFACE

The Call To Spiritual Sonship

The inspiration of this writing began many years ago. At that time being a child of God was not clear to me as much as it has now become. My recommitment to receiving Christ in my life as a young adult became a turning point I could not have imagined until now. I was blessed with being placed in a church community rooted in biblical truths and principals that changed my life forever. As I continued to give myself to the things of God, I began to sense the urgency for submitting to the Lordship of Jesus although I wasn't quite sure where it would lead. With time, I began to see the need of others, like myself, to experience God in a meaningful way. The desire to help others was further developed in me. The more I read and gave myself to the word of God the greater was my desire for helping others. As time went on, given the opportunity to serve in various capacities, I learned my true desire was to know God in a way I'd never known possible. These opportunities in serving seemed to me to be affirmations of spiritual success. However, I would soon learn that they were not indicative of the true relationship I had longed to be confident in. Even as I continued to yield to the environment of the scriptures, I had no real sense of capturing the elusive power and presence of the Holy Spirit that I read about in the scriptures. My frustrations became evident with my intolerance for messages that did not give specific guidance into this relationship. In more recent years I have come to know the Lord in ways that have led into the relationship that I longed for and knew was possible. Through many seasons of spiritual growth, my pursuit of God's presence has made me realize His unique care for me. As God speaks to me it is through the sound of the voice of a father. This sound is like rain. He declares, "Let my teaching fall like rain and my words descend like dew, like showers on new grass, like abundant rain on tender plants." (Deut. 32: 2) Through the preached word, study of the scriptures and guidance of the Holy Spirit, God has unveiled Himself to me and let me know that He is my Father. In my search for God's presence He's made me aware of the process revealed in sonship that He has prepared for those who desire to know Him. (Isaiah 42:6A) This process is through The Lord Jesus Christ as the Son, the way, the truth, and the light of God the Father. The revelation of the knowledge of Christ, as the firstborn of many spiritual sons has become the bread I needed to consume. (Col. 1:5, Heb. 2:19, Rom. 8:29) I'm finding the truth of who I am in God is locked up in the knowledge of the Son. "But in these last days he has spoken to us by his Son..." (Hebrews 1:2). As I have looked at the scriptures from a Christo-centric perspective with Christ being the central theme for my case study, God has shown me (2 Cor. 5:21) "To those who believed in his name, he gave the right to become children of God" (John 1:12), "I pray that the eyes of your heart may be enlightened that you may know..." (Ephesians 1:18) This implies that sons must have a father capable of bringing the son into the inheritance given of the Father. I now understand that every covenantal promise for me has been given to me as a son, not as an orphan. My responsibility for receiving my inheritance in Christ is to recognize the Son as the one sent to lead me in the righteousness of God, how God has established our relationship to Him as sons. (John 7:16) What has been stirred in my spirit is a need to sound the call for spiritual sons to be mentored and configured, into righteousness by spiritual fathers. God has given the spirit of sonship to the righteous in Christ. (1Peter 3:18). Sons can only move beyond the elementary things of Christ through a father son wineskin relationship. Sons are matured as they experience the complete expression of relationship through submission to a father modeling the righteousness of Christ (Hebrews 6:1-3, 2 Cor.5: 21).

INTRODUCTION

One of the most important aspects of Jesus' ministry was to show the world the Father's love. Seeded within the purpose of the church is its responsibility to birth and nurture sons of God. "All this is from God, who reconciled us to himself through Christ and **gave us the ministry of reconciliation**: that God was reconciling the world to himself in Christ, not counting people's sins against them. And he has committed to us the **message** of reconciliation. We are therefore ambassadors, **as though God were making His appeal through us.**" (2Cor. 5:18-20). As the second Adam and **firstborn** son, Jesus was given the assignment of "bringing many sons and daughters to glory," (Hebrews 2:10). Jesus acknowledged in a prayer for his disciples that God the Father had given authority to give eternal life to all the Father gave him (John 17:2). For this view to be understood we must see Jesus as the carrier of this truth in how his historical and ascended life modeled the Father' intent. In the last day prophecy to Malachi, God spoke of sending the spirit of Elijah to institute a return of the father's heart to children and the children's hearts would return to their fathers. When Elisha witnessed Elijah's departure he cried out "My father, my father" (II Kings 2). This instance was a prophetic picture of a son recognizing his spiritual father' assignment in the earth and sought his mantle of spiritual inheritance. Elijah represented to Elisha the spirit of fatherhood. When Adam sinned he became separated from his father, God, and God sent the spirit of Fatherhood through Jesus Christ "The Everlasting Father". The principle of father is that you will see in the natural father, ways and representations characteristic of the heavenly Father. Through God's spirit the human father will be given the grace to model the character of God. The purpose of this declaration was God addressing in His foreknowledge the curse of an irreverent generation that rejects the authority of a father.

Elijah's role in Elisha's life was as a spiritual father, called of God to give Elisha an inheritance meant for him by God. Elisha's natural father could not give to Elisha what Elijah was ordained to do and that was to point Elisha to God the Father. The relationship between this father/son imagery underscores the principle of transference and representation. Without Elijah, Elisha would not have fulfilled his purpose and without

Elisha's submission or Elijah's seeking Elisha, Elijah would have failed in the most important part of his call to be a spiritual father. The resounding alarm for the church today is for it to respond to the establishment of true fathers within the houses of God so sons can be birthed, nurtured, and given their rightful inheritances of Sonship in God. (2 Cor. 5:18-20) God is not about building ministries that showcase the charisma of one individual's ability to serve the masses. Jesus said, "the poor you will have with you always". He was speaking to those who like Martha, were able to recognize the importance of ministering to His will. Jesus came to do the work of His Father and that was to reconcile sons back unto His Father. Jesus' mandate was to be "the first of many brethren".

The signs today in the world communicate a dire picture of a world reeling from the lack of leadership or headship impacting governments, institutions, societies, homes, and unfortunately the church. This absence of leadership is showing a spirit of apathy that has become the source for cold, loveless groupthink amidst the population. Unfortunately, this same spirit has found its way into the church where traditionalism and denominationalism continues to be the religious focus. Current events, of late, have caught the attention of the world and many are wondering what these signs mean. The increase of global calamities has gripped the attention and focus of the masses. The initial response to these outbreaks has not been sufficient to impede the spread of hysteria therefore the impact has caused great alarm. Through dysfunctional responses and communication, world governments have found themselves unable to get a handle on these situations that would normally have been mitigated through standardized protocols. The apparent disruptions have become evident through hyper-politicized, nationalistic, and economically poor environments leaving thousands dying, becoming homeless, jobless, and without healthcare in the wake of leaders abdicating their responsibilities to the public. "Woe to you, O land, when your king is a child and your princes feast in the morning! (Ecclesiastes 10: 16) The church's response during this time is under considerable review because the world is lost for answers. The response to natural needs such as food, clothing, and shelter are all felt needs that are characteristic of the natural poor. But, there is a spiritually poor individual lost because of the distractions of the carnal nature. The signs of what is the effects of floods, earthquakes, and wildfires all speak to another seismic shifting taking place, and that is the spiritual movements of God. God meant to create man in His image and likeness. Since God is spirit, in the image of God, man is also spirit. Therefore, the nature and substance of man, like God, is spirit. Man is spirit because God gave out of His person the spirit that He breathed into man. However the likeness of God is different because the likeness represents the nature and character of God. God is righteous therefore His sons must be righteous also. (Ps. 119:137). These attributes must be discipled into the person who is to represent another (2 Cor. 5:21). This is the reason why the home is so important. The home is where one grows up to be like their father in learning the attitude and character of the father. God birthed the church through Christ so that in His house sons of God would be exposed to spiritual fathers reflecting His likeness.

Foundational to the prophecy in Malachi, God has brought back emphasis of the apostolic position in the church. The apostle is an oracle who speaks as a mouthpiece for God. In the Old Testament the apostle is a patriarch, one who establishes an ordinance, precept, regulation, or command of God. They were also known as an "apostolos" or a sent one. This gift over the years has been interpreted through hierarchal context rather than the grace of a pattern design builder. Only through the eyes of the Holy Spirit can this grace be truly understood as it benefits the foundation of true sons. Jesus being the chief apostle and cornerstone was sent to speak as the Father and demonstrate the fullness of the father's grace. As "The Everlasting Father", Jesus brings into the new covenant all of the present truths of the ancient biblical patterns given for the building of God's house and family. The reinstitution of apostolic doctrine according to divine biblical patterns is the prerequisite essential for the building up of sons in the house of God. The function of apostles is to lay the foundation of identity and function or behavior of godly sons. The pillars of Acts 2: 42 lay out the building blocks for spiritual engagement of a healthy church environment under the leadership of the Holy Spirit. This is important because these pillars establish the truth of relationship, fellowship, and grace given of the Father to sons of inheritance. Divine Sonship is rooted in three immutable principles where God has mandated sons in the earth. The Firstborn principle establishes the right of status as a son through the seed of Abraham, birthed in the faith of the death, burial, and resurrection of Jesus Christ. Second, the royal priesthood designation speaks of the son's right as spiritual leaders chosen to stand before God on behalf of the family and representing God in the earth. Lastly, as brethren of the "king of kings and Lord of Lords", all sons of God are kings in the earth representing the kingdom authority of Christ given by God the Father. These principles must be embraced by a church generation that is able to concretely conceptualize the depth and power attributed to this truth. Therefore sound apostolic doctrine must be given, received, and implemented for the inheritance of God to be manifested. "The Call To Spiritual Sonship" is a heavenly inspired response to what is a clear mandate for sounding an alarm for true sons to emerge within the church. Obviously sons can only come forth when fathers take their place. This work in writing is only a part of what is seen and needing to be proclaimed as loudly and as often as possible.

STAGES OF SPIRITUAL SONSHIP

Nepios

Infant, baby not old enough to speak or function

Born Again – "For you have been born again, not of perishable seed, but of imperishable, through the living and enduring Word of God". (1 Peter 1:23)

Paidon

Little child able to understand some Godly Principles

Child of God

"To them He gave the right to become the children of God." (John 1:12)

Teknon Teenager beginning to want to understand his/her own destiny.

Sons of God

"So that by the grace of God he might taste death for everyone, in bringing many Sons and daughters to glory". (Hebrews 2:9c-10)

Neaniskos

Young Adult beginning to rule his/her own life well.

Huios Fully matured son who represents his father well.

Beloved…

"This is My Beloved Son, in whom I am well pleased." (Matthew 3:17)

Pater

This son embodies the Father expressly as one given to the exact representation of the Father's will, modeling this position for other fathers to emulate. "I am writing to you fathers because you know Him who has been from the beginning." (1 John 2: 13a)

"Just as you know how we were exhorting and encouraging and imploring each one of you as a father would his own children, so that you would walk in a manner worthy of the

God who calls you into His own kingdom and glory." (1 Thess. 2: 11,12)

THE NEPIOS SON

Greek definitions:

Zodhiates: "One who cannot speak, hence an infant, child limited in age"

<u>Spiros Zodhiates - Wikipedia</u> en.wikipedia.org/wiki/Spiros_Zodhiates)

Strong: "An infant; figuratively, a simple-minded person; immature".(*Strong, James (1890), <u>The Exhaustive Concordance of the Bible</u>, Cincinnati: Jennings & Graham).*

Thayer: "Little, child, childish, untaught, unskilled". <u>(Joseph Henry Thayer - Wikipedia</u> en.wikipedia.org/wiki/Joseph_Henry_Thayer)

(Note) The Greek term BREPHOS – babies is akin to NEPIOS

"like newborn babies long for the pure milk of the word so that by it you may grow in respect to salvation." (1 Peter 2:2)

Nepios: infant

This infant baby is not old enough to speak or function. A nepios individual is young in the spiritual things of God. After accepting Jesus as the Son of God and receiving in faith the forgiveness of their sins through the finished work of Christ on the cross, this person must begin the journey of laying in their lives the foundation truths of the gospel. The best way for this is being connected to a local house of God that has a solid kingdom culture in place. The new believer must start the process of identifying with their new life in Christ and this is done through establishing new ways of thinking and behaving. As with all believers, adherence to God's word becomes the strength of a nepios's new walk. The word encourages a mental transformation (Romans 12: 2) through adopting the scriptural view of the purpose for allowing Jesus the Lordship in our lives. As a babe in Christ, it's important for the nepios to have a solid concept of their new identity. This means that like a child learning new things relative to their individual self, a nepios believer should seek to know their identity in Christ and how they are viewed as children of God. A nepios must understand their rights as a child of God. (John 1: 12) Under consistent spiritual instruction, encouragement and guidance in the word of God, a nepios individual can successfully bridge their faith to the resurrected life in the word. Through the use of spiritual tutors such as those who serve in local ministry, the nepios can find help in establishing a faithful walk in Christ. Healthy kingdom environments teach the nepios the importance of doctrinal truths that undergird their faith. The more a nepios exposes themselves to authentic ministry characterized by apostolic doctrine, the greater likelihood of their success to grow in "desiring the sincere milk of the word". (1 Peter 2:2) During the initial engrafting stage of a believer, God will guide them through heartfelt yearnings to become attached to a local fellowship. This step is one where God is placing the child in a house for their spiritual training. Usually the lead servant of the house along with others more established in their walk, they become a support to the nepios. "And He gave some apostles, and some as prophets, and some as evangelists, and some as pastors and teachers for the equipping of the saints for the work of the service, to the building up of the body of Christ, until we all attain to the unity of the faith, and of the knowledge of the Son of God, to the measure of the stature which belongs to the fullness of Christ." (Ephesians 4: 11-13) The benefit of apostolic doctrine to a nepios cannot be underestimated for its importance of establishing the right foundation for building the needed spiritual disciplines. When a nepios is under such truth that encourages and displays consistent kingdom culture, spiritual growth can be expected and encouraged.

"As a result, we are no longer to be children tossed here and there by waves and carried about by every wind of doctrine, by the trickery of men, by craftiness in deceitful scheming; but speaking the truth in love, we are to grow up in all aspects into Him who is the head, even Christ, from whom the whole body, being fitted and held together by what every joint supplies according to the proper working of each individual part, causes the growth of the body for the building up of itself in love" (Ephesians 4: 14-16).

The impact of authentic apostolic ministry promotes the relational dynamic of spiritual fathering because of its inherent graces. Jesus modeled the fathering grace to the disciples in bringing them to the truth of sonship. Likewise, ministry towards a nepios son should always reflect a father/son dynamic of the son pursued in relationship by the father. The father's goal towards the son is to point the son to Christ through his modeling of the character of the Father. Like natural children, it's not uncommon for a child to develop a preference or bias towards an individual they perceive as helpful. What must be avoided with nepios sons is an idolized attitude that hinders the son's ability to hear God in any other voice God may use. "For when one says, "I am of Paul," and another, "I am of Apollos," are you not mere men? (1Corinthians 3: 4) This situation can hinder the growth of the son and be a trap of the enemy. Care should always be taken to discern any word given. However, a son is never too young to desire the sincere truth by judging what's being said. Spiritual fathers help sons rightly divide the word of truth when it's necessary. The sooner a nepios is encouraged to exercise their spiritual senses they must do so. Commitment to this discipline will wean them from the milk and allow them to take on the meat of the word. Nepios sons may find themselves prone to carnal proclivities because they are being transformed as they continue walking with Christ. Past behaviors are more familial responses to old ways of thinking and doing but regaining the power of self-will is able to alleviate these issues. The goal for nepios sons is to solidify their identity by pursuing the truth of who they are in Christ. The more the knowledge of Christ is known, the more a nepios is able to function appropriately in the family of God. Through application of the kingdom culture, in shared values, beliefs and perspectives, the nepios can experience expressions of divine love. This love becomes in them an organic expression of the influence of the Holy Spirit.

(Hebrews 5:13- 6:3)

"For everyone who partakes only of milk is unskilled in the word of righteousness, for he is a babe (nepios). But solid food belongs to those who are of full age (teleios), that is those who by reason of use have their senses exercised to discern both good and evil. Therefore, leaving the discussion of the elementary principles of Christ, let us go on to perfection, not laying again the foundation of repentance from dead works and of faith toward God. Of the doctrine of baptisms, of the laying on of hands, of resurrection of the dead, and of eternal judgment, and this we will do if God permits."

(Hebrews 5: 12 – 6:3)

"For though by this time you ought to be teachers, you need someone to teach you again the first principles of the oracles of God; and you have come to need milk and not solid food." The writer of Hebrews contrasts two positions relating to two specific levels of spiritual development, which are described as a foundation position on the one hand characteristic of the 'nepios' son and the 'mature' position on the other, characteristic of the 'huios' son. Below are these two positions contrasted using the phrases in the text quoted above :

Foundation Position (Nepois}	Mature Position
A Babe Hebrews – 5:13	Full Age - Hebrews 5:14
Milk Hebrews - 5:12	Solid Food - Hebrews 5:14
Students Teach You – Hebrews 5:12	Teachers - Hebrews 5:12
First or Elementary Principles – Hebrews 5: 12;6:1	Going on to Perfection – Hebrews 6:1
Inexperienced/Unskilled in the word - Hebrews 5:13	Practiced in the word – Hebrews 5:14

We are never to stagnate spiritually but to always progress toward ultimate perfection in God. The Hebrew Christians seemed to have plateaued out at a specific level of spiritual growth indicated by the 'foundation position' in the illustration above. The writer of Hebrews exhorts them to reinforce the foundation of the elementary or basic principles of Christ and then to consciously LEAVE this position to proceed to maturity. Contextually then, the nepios son is characterized by inconsistency of personal engagement with the Word of God, and an inability to receive a weightier or meatier Word because he has not mastered the elementary doctrines of Christ listed in **Heb. 6:1-2**, both in understanding and as a lifestyle practice. Also, he is 'unskilled' in the Word of righteousness, i.e. he is inexperienced in both accurately dividing the Word of Truth, and having failed to practically apply the Word thus becoming subjectively and personally inexperienced in the 'Word of righteousness'. Doctrine is profitable for training in righteousness (**2 Tim. 3:16**) and must be fully demonstrated in his life. This level of growth has the subtle effect of not having a developed or heightened sense of discernment of good and evil, - which is something that only comes through habitual and consistent engagement of one's spiritual faculties (actively engaging your spirit through the Holy Spirit). Foundational to a healthy nepios is establishing a consistent practice of spiritual disciplines incorporating habits that promote a deep love for doctrine and for the Word of God. The study and practice of the Word of God with greater consistency creates a platform for transformation in thought and deed. Mastering the elementary doctrines of **Hebrews 6:1,2** enables the new believer to comprehend with clarity the knowledge of what has been done to secure their redemption. As you exercise your spiritual senses, discernment begins to happen with greater regularity (by reason of use – **Heb.5: 13**). "When I was a child, I used to speak like a child, think like a child, reason like a child; when I became a man, *I DID AWAY WITH CHILDISH THINGS.*" (1 Cor. 13:11)' **did away with**'= *katargeo*= to render idle, inactive or inoperative, to cause a thing to have no further efficiency; to deprive of force, influence and power; to cause to cease; to put an end to; to annul, to abolish; to be severed or separated from; to terminate intercourse with. As we grow spiritually we must deliberately '**PUT AWAY**' childish talk, reasoning and any other behavior. As indicated above, the Greek counterpart of this phrase implies a conscious setting aside and reducing to total inactivity any proclivity, or tendency to revert to childish ways and thinking. As a new believer the process of learning new ways of behaving is akin to a child mastering walking, talking or thinking. Through intentional or willful decisions to guard conscious expressive behaviors, frivolous actions can be avoided. Note in the passage above, this happens 'when we become 'a man' – i.e. mature. You will naturally outgrow certain childish thought patterns and behaviors as you proceed toward maturity.

THE PAIDON

Greek Definitions:

Strong: "Half grown boy/ girl, figuratively, 'immature'."

Thayer: "A little child; a more advanced child; metaphorically –children in intellect"

Paidon – A little child mature enough to understand and proclaim. The paidon child of God has matured beyond nepios enough to recognize the character and nature of the Father, knowing both His intimacy and sovereignty becomes a priority. The paidon son is fundamentally established in the basics of redemptive truth. As a nepios they learned the significance of relating the word to themselves specifically. This son has become comfortable with receiving from the hand of God through the ways provided. As a son with a bit more understanding of the blessings of kingdom culture and how it impacts the life of a believer, this stage stirs the heart. Even though the new life in Christ is not without its challenges the joys of knowing God's love brings a peace. The paidon is more consistent in applying the word and through trial and error they find the faith of others to be a comfort. This shared faith creates a bond and allows for intimacy to develop personally in their journey with God as Father.

As a spiritual toddler, the paidon should be able to walk steady. This pace is one of identifying rights and privileges, understanding their decision-making and the importance of their spiritual heritage. The lessons of the scripture woven into the history of the patriarchs and how God established them becomes of great importance. Continuing in their maturation process with the help of a spiritual father, the paidon becomes equipped to handle inherent weaknesses of the flesh. They understand the word written as commands guarding against attacks of the enemy. The diligent paidon is not easily deterred due to lapses in doubts because they realize their journey is a race and not a sprint. They become familiar with the "wilderness" principle knowing that they too have a journey within their transformation in submitting to the word. In this stage diligence manifests a growth in wisdom and favor. Through observance the paidon witnesses the grace of God on the lives of others. They can be sparked to begin to sense a purpose or desire to serve in an area they find passion for. The increase of spiritual disciplines such as reading the word daily, meditating upon the word, giving time to sit before the Lord in prayerful silence and being open to times of depriving the flesh to gain spiritual energy; these become a joy. During this stage the son's interest in spiritual things intensifies to where they began to desire the work of the Father, receiving the one He sends. During this season of gaining insight the child will be in a place to begin to receive the Father's grace on his life. For the first time he really begins to enter/ experience the Kingdom of the Father. In this season the child grows in strength, wisdom, and grace. (In the natural paidon describes a child between 2-10 years old)

Key Verses: (1 John 2:13, Matt. 19:13, Matt. 18:2-5, Luke 2: 34-40, 1 Cor. 14:20)

"I am writing to you, little children (teknon), because your sins have been forgiven you for His name's sake. I am writing to you, fathers, because you know Him who has been from the beginning. I am writing to you, young men (neaniskos), because you have overcome the evil one. I have written to you, children (paidon), because you know the Father." (1 John 2:12,13)

THE PAIDON

As in the natural when a child begins to develop an appreciation of their parents that stems from a perceived intimacy, a loving nature defines the relationship beyond the aspects of protection, provision and preservation. Through recognition and awareness, the child internally perceives a privilege and blessing being born to such a loving parent or parents. The child develops an appreciation of their parents beyond what is done for them and this in turn is similar to the spiritual process of a paidon son towards the Heavenly Father. As the paidon becomes aware of the blessings of his walk in God, he also is accepting of the challenges to implement kingdom culture.

" Then some children were brought to Him so that He might lay His hands on them and pray; and the disciples rebuked them. But Jesus said, "Let the children alone, and do not hinder them from coming to "Me" for the Kingdom of Heaven belongs to such as these." After laying His hands on them, He departed from there." (Matthew 19:13)

The paidon son understands his blessings in Christ as God's Son. (Eph. 1:3, Gal. 3:8; Deut. 28) Humbling challenges become a sign of growth for the paidon son. Humility includes being meek and gentle, which are traits of the heart our Lord expects of all His disciples learning of Him. (Matt. 11: 28-30) Humility (prautes) is "mildness of disposition, gentleness of spirit and meekness". Humility requires the paidon to seek out their journey to being contrite earnestly. Recognizing the hindrances of pride, childlike faith in humility gains entrance into the kingdom expressions of life. He learns to deal with the pride of life.

"And He called a child to Himself and set him before them, and said, "Truly I say to you, unless you are converted and become like children, you will not enter the kingdom of heaven" Whosoever then humbles himself as this child, he is the greatest in the kingdom of heaven. And whoever receives one such child in My name, receives Me." (Matthew 18: 2-5)

The paidon embraces the culture of Kingdom, receiving the precepts of the word establishing a heavenly perspective about life.

"Truly I say to you, whoever does not receive the kingdom of God like a child will not enter it at all." (Mark 10:15)

At this stage the paidon son engages the reading and study of the Word of God (apostolic doctrine) more consistently and enthusiastically, growing in spiritual stature, wisdom and grace. Important to note here is the emphasis on coming before the word with a childlike trusting nature. This trusting disposition expresses itself in the non-hesitant obedience to God's commands. The piadon son begins to silence the voice of reason and logic from the domain of the unregenerate areas of his soul, and simply obeys from the platform of his spirit. This son starts to learn unswerving trust and faith from commitment in compliance to God's word and ways. The increase in strength, wisdom and grace is marked by a deliberate pursuit of the paidon to maintain a habitual discipline of applying faith and obedience. This word is used to describe Jesus from approximately 2 years to about 11 years old. " The Child (paidon) continued to grow and became strong, increasing in wisdom; and the grace of God was upon Him." (Luke 2:40)

(Note) At twelve years old, Mary addressed Jesus as 'teknon' (Luke 2:48).

At that time Jesus had an awareness that He must be about His Father's business and thought He was ready for the task. However after a reprimand by his earthly spiritual parents (Joseph and Mary), He subjected Himself to them another 18 years and emerged at 30 years old as a mature Son. The transition from nepios to paidon, teknon and ultimately huios can potentially be a phase where many sons of God make shipwreck of their calling in God. Premature engagement with one's calling out of zeal or ambition can be disastrous, hence the need for the son to submit to the oversight of spiritual fathering. The child still needs development in his thinking, especially in how to practically apply the gifts, talents and abilities the Lord has given him.

" Brethren, do not be children (paidon) in your thinking; yet in evil be infants (nepiazo), but in your thinking be mature (teleios)." (1 Cor. 14:20) 'Nepiazo' implies innocence in the context above; 'Teleios' means mature, perfect or complete. While the paidon son exhibits knowledge of developing intimacy with the Father, and can understand certain spiritual operations within the Kingdom and Church, his spiritual mental faculties are not completely or fully developed and as such needs greater maturation to the perfect state. The context of 1 Cor. 14 concerns the practical administration of the gifts of prophecy and speaking in tongues and interpretation of tongues. Paul appeals for a mature (teleios) mindset in how this is done, especially when determining the appropriateness of the exercise of these gifts dependent on the context or environment. The son may have gifts but lack wisdom to effectively administrate them. The paidon may at times have difficulty understanding the will of God in his life during a specific season and this is where spiritual mentoring is critical. The Emmaus principle offers one of the more important opportunities for a paidon to navigate these times. This principle calls for the paidon to have another older believer walk alongside them in their journey helping them to evaluate the word as it impacts their lives with sober eyes.

(Take time to read the entire chapter of John 21)

"But when the day was now breaking, Jesus stood on the beach; yet the disciples did not know that it was Jesus. So Jesus said to them, " Children (paidon), you do not have any fish, do you?" They answered Him, "No". And He said to them, " Cast the net on the right hand side of the boat and you will catch." So they cast, and then they were not able to haul it in because of the great number of fish." (John 21: 4-6)

Jesus after His resurrection appeared to His disciples who went fishing. He called them 'paidon' alluding to the fact that they had reverted to a wrong preoccupation (fishing). For one they failed to understand how the will of God was playing itself out. Two, they failed to comprehend how and where Christ was to be recognized, revealed and understood in the current disclosure of Himself to the earth, and three they failed to discern the dealings of God with them in that season of their lives. Hence they, in discouragement, went back to their previous employment, one in which they could not manifest any fruit (no fish), until they reconnected with the risen Christ.

At times the paidon son will not fully understand a specific season of his life or how God is dealing with him in that season, especially in reference to God's purposes for him and how this should play itself out. More so, it might seem as if the Lord has abandoned the son, for the son is somewhat unaccustomed to the new revelation of Christ that is wanting to break through to his mind in this time. Failure to fully understand these things can cause discouragement in the son; creating a sense of futility in regards to the time he has given himself to God's ways and will, and deeming that all this has amounted to nothing (for the disciples it was three years). He may abandon his calling in God and the vigor with which he pursues it, although he is still in relationship with God. He might pursue a previous preoccupation or 'lesser' engagement (as in 'fishing') with little or no fruit of divine favor on it (having caught no fish). Jesus did not rebuke the disciples for reverting to previous ways of seeking to fulfill their ideas of work. He instead issued a command to them telling them where to cast their nets. In doing so the disciples were rewarded with a large catch of fish, so large they could barely hold the catch. In response to obeying what they perceived as a familiar voice, the disciples retrieve 153 large fish which represents in Jewish Gamatria 'mega sonship or mature sonship' reflecting the standard or level of sonship they were called to by Jesus Christ. John recognizes the Lord as does Peter, and he re-mantles himself in his garment; only obedience to the voice of Jesus can bring forth such results. The re-robing Peter does is symbolic of recommitment to the apostolic mandate given them by Jesus as His followers. Jesus then challenges Peter concerning the feeding of His lambs, the caring of His sheep and the feeding of His sheep. Peter along with the rest, hear the familiar command of Jesus, "Follow Me".

At times God may respond with great provision in order to teach the paidon son who is called to significant levels of commitment to God's purposes (as Peter was). God may teach him that He will take care of him and that he need not revert to dependence on his own way to provide for his own need. This great divine provision accomplishes much more than this. It signifies to the son the great love and mercy of the Father. It evokes a response within the son to resist distraction, and to wholeheartedly pursue God's will at any cost. (This is evidenced in John 21 where Jesus unveils to Peter the type of death he would die and Peter's willingness to still follow the Lord in spite of this).

THE TEKNON SON

The main usage of this word stresses the fact of a spiritual birth and relationship with God.

Greek Definitions:

Strong: "A child" (as produced)

Zodhiates: "True children, genuine descendants"

When God promised Abraham his seed would be blessed, Abraham replied "Lord what can you give me since I remain childless and the one who will inherit my estate is Eliezer of Damascus?" (Genesis 15: 2-4) In this exchange Abraham is concerned about having a son blessed who is not of his flesh. God tells him he will have a son from his own body. Abraham received this promise from God in spite of his and Sarah's age, and God imputed to him a righteous standing because of his belief in God's word. Abraham received all of his sons in faith and this made him a father of spiritual sons. The Teknon understands he is a spiritual son of faith who is born to another. (John 8:39; 1 Pet. 3:6)

According to Thayer the name teknon transforms the intimate and reciprocal relationship formed by the bonds of love, trust and friendship.

Teknon – A pupil or disciple who is instructed by their teacher to nourish their minds and mold their character. Every Son of God should be passionate about their ability to bring the will of God into the earth on every level. This should be done in marriage, relationships, workplaces with superiors, subordinates, and peers. How we relate to each other in the body of Christ, in our houses of worship, to our leader and other leaders and houses that flow in different streams of truth is also important. At every level we want to see the will of the Lord done. In John 3: 34 Jesus said, " My food is to do the will of Him who sent me to accomplish His work." Jesus had this priority within Him to do the will of God, his Father. Jesus said the Father's will was his food or meat. As in Hebrews 6: 5, food or meat is the mature doctrine whereas milk is the elementary word of God. While food is nourishment to the natural body, Jesus was saying that doing the will of God the Father was the energy or nourishment to his body. God is bringing compliancy and alignment into His kingdom in the earth. "...in all the will of God." (Col.4: 12) Encouraged to develop their mind spiritually, the teknon senses a heightened desire for looking deeper into the principles of the word. This is a time he embraces the birthright of the son and finds his place in his spiritual lineage and heritage. At this stage, this child begins to identify the ways of his Father's business. This child receives the trans-generational promises and understands the altar of spiritual sacrifices of dying to self. This child matures quickly as he nurtures a lifestyle of sacrifice. During this season the depth of wisdom, stature, and favor are mitigated by the son's ability to empathize with others seeking to reflect the father's image. Love for others flourishes during this season.

(In the natural this describes a spiritual child between 10-17 years old)

Key Verses: (1 John 2:12, 2:1, 3:18, 3:10; John 13:13; Ephesians 5:1; Luke 2:46-52; Romans 9:6-8; Galatians 4:28,31)

This son is fully conscious that his sins have been forgiven and that condemnation has no place in his thought life. This child knows he is forgiven and his forgiveness of others gives way to grace in his life. Because he has accepted Jesus as his advocate with the Father, he is learning to love not just in speech but in deeds also.

"And they brought to Him a paralytic lying on a bed. Seeing their faith, Jesus said to the paralytic, "Take courage, son (*teknon*); your sins are forgiven." (Matthew 9:2)

"I am writing to you, little children (*teknon*) because your sins have been forgiven you for His name's sake." (1 John 2:12)

Note: 'teknion' is the diminutive form of 'teknon'.

At this stage the son is no longer paralyzed by feelings of guilt and condemnation from their weaknesses. Just as Jesus encouraged Peter when he said, " Satan desires to sift you as wheat but I have prayed for you", he understands the inherent strength and grace of their Father to impute righteousness to them as they pursue His provision of forgiveness for weaknesses. (Romans 6:1-2; Hebrews 9:14; Psalms 32:1,2) The teknon has received the legitimate and valid relationship with his Father through deliberate review of the scriptures. The son knows their rightful position as sons of God and strives wholeheartedly to walk as such. Reception of Christ qualifies one legally and officially to be a part of His family. In a technical sense this son recognizes, "Christ redeemed us from the curse of the law by becoming a curse for us, for it is written: "Cursed is everyone who is hung on a tree." (Galatians 3:13) The emphasis in John 1: 12 is not so much upon the stage of development as in a child. Rather the Son of God has the Right to be called so. In this sense, in which it is used, sonship stresses the issue that a legal, legitimate relationship exists with God. The teknon like Jesus will began to desire to respond to the commands of the Father and follow his example. In faith the teknon knows that Jesus' relationship with God as Father, is in fact his own position with the Father. The teknon recognizes he is like Isaac, a child of promise born of the free woman.

"But it is not as though the word of God has failed. For they are not all Israel who are descended from Israel, nor are they all children (*teknon*) because they are Abraham's descendants; but "through Isaac your descendants shall be named". That is, it is not the children of the flesh who are children (*teknon*) of God, but the children of promise who are regarded as descendants. (Romans 9:6-8)

"He came to His own, and those who were His own did not receive Him. But as many as received Him, to them He gave the right to become children (*teknon*) of God, even to those who believe in His name, who were born, not of blood nor of the will of the flesh nor of the will of man, but of God" (John 1: 11,12). Teknon also denotes the sense of someone understanding they are a part of a specific lineage or dynasty. The natural descendants of Abraham were not the Israel of God, but rather anyone who, like Isaac was, is a son of promise through Christ. "He redeemed us in order that the blessing given to Abraham might come to the gentiles through Christ Jesus, so that by faith we might receive the promise of the Spirit." (Galatians 3: 14) The teknon has the witness of the Spirit within him that he is a legitimate Son of God. "The Spirit Himself testifies with our spirit that we are children (*teknon*) of God." (Romans 8:16)

The teknon son starts to practice a life of mortifying the flesh overcoming sin and expressing practical righteousness. "For we know that our old self was crucified with him so that the body ruled by sin might be done away with, that we should no longer beslaves to sin..." "Therefore do not let sin reign in your mortal body so that you obey its evil desires." (Romans 6: 6, 12) The maturity of the teknon is evident in the way they have developed a mind that places the truth of God about who they are as primary. In spite of the wiles of the enemy, the teknon has grown in their use of spiritual truth to defeat the accusations of the devil.

"My little children (*teknon*), I am writing these things to you so that you may not sin. And if anyone sins, we have an advocate with the Father, Jesus Christ the righteous." (1 John 2:1)

"By this the children (*teknon*) of God and the children of the devil are obvious, anyone who does not practice righteousness is not of God, nor the one who does not love his brother." (1 John 3:10)

The son's ability to demonstrate the love of the Father flourishes in love for others. In other words, they see the preordained covenant love of God for all. "For I am convinced that neither death nor life, neither angels nor demons, neither the present nor the future, nor any powers, neither height nor depth, nor anything else in all creation, will be able to separate us from the love of God that is in Christ Jesus our Lord." (Romans 8: 38-39) Pursuant to these words the teknon sees love as the primary element of God's nature and faithfulness as a father to those He loves.

"Little children (*teknon*), let us not love with word or tongue, but in deed and truth." (1 John 3:18)

"Therefore be imitators of God, as beloved children (*teknon*), and walk in love just as Christ also loved you and gave Himself up for us, an offering and a sacrifice to God as a fragrant aroma." (Ephesians 5:1,2)

The son submits his own ambitions and will in subjection to a spiritual father, who through instruction of the Word exemplifies the nature of Christ within him, thus facilitating his rapid progression to maturity – and a four-dimensional growth in stature, wisdom, favor with God and favor with men.

"Then, after three days they found Him in the temple, sitting in the midst of the teachers, both listening to them and asking them questions. And all who heard Him were amazed at the understanding and His answers. When they saw Him, they were astonished; and His mother said to Him, "Son (*teknon*) why have you treated us this way? Behold your father and I have been anxiously looking for you", and He said to them, "Why is it that you were looking for me? Did you not know that I had to be in My Father's house? But they did not understand the statement, which He had made to them. And He went down with them and came to Nazareth, and He continued in subjection to them, and His mother treasured all these things in her heart. And Jesus kept increasing in wisdom and stature, and in favor with God and men." (Luke 2:46-52)

Jesus at this stage was aware that He had a calling and had to be about His Father's business. He demonstrated great knowledge and understanding such that well schooled teachers of His day were astonished at His listening skills and comprehension capacity, His probing questions, and the wisdom and insight He exhibited by the answers He provided. Yet all of this was still insufficient to fully release Him into a practical expression of His Father's will. He had to be in subjection to spiritual parents as represented in Joseph and Mary, who put His life in right alignment – (as suggested by the Greek word 'hupotasso' translated as subjection). The spiritual father labors to form Christ fully within his spiritual son. Even though Joseph was Jesus' earthly father, he stood in representation to Jesus as the patriarchal order of blessed authority. Joseph was no less a father in spirit because he was the model of a father who recognized God as Lord.

"My children (*teknon*) with whom I am again in labor until Christ be formed in you." (Colossians 1: 28,29)

"We proclaim Him, admonishing every man and teaching every man with all wisdom, so that we may present every man complete in Christ. For this purpose also I labor, striving according to His power, which mightily works within me." Paul used the term often to describe his spiritual son Timothy. (2

Tim. 1:2; 1 Tim. 1:2; 1 Cor. 4:17; Phil. 2: 22) Many believe in this context that it is also a term of endearment and love. It highlights the teacher/learner relationship between the father and son. The teknon should have an active learning experience with the Father through his spiritual father. Consider how Eli trained Samuel to discern God's voice: 1 Samuel 3: 16 "The Lord called yet again, "Samuel". So Samuel arose and went to Eli and said, "Here I am, for you called me" but he answered, "I did not call, my son, lie down again." Participation in a father/son relationship helps the son to learn how to hear the voice of the Lord. The spiritual father can teach and guide the son through the process of developing a listening ear that is able to distinguish God's voice within the voice of those He chooses to speak for Him.

A teknon must walk closely in doctrine marking the ways of his spiritual father in the Lord during this time. "Follow my example, as I follow the example of Christ." (1 Cor. 11:1) Probably more than any other time, it is imperative that the teknon mimic the ways of the spiritual father, so long as these are reflective of Christ in every way.

"Therefore be imitators of God, as beloved children (*teknon*) and walk in love, just as Christ also loved you and gave Himself up for us, an offering and sacrifice to God as a fragrant aroma."

(Ephesians 5:1,2) Imitators = mimetes = followers – we get the English word mimic from this word – i.e. it relates to copying exactly. By imitating the ways and doctrine of an accurate and credible spiritual father in the Lord who has or is connected to an authentic apostolic grace, the son is actually imitating God Himself.

"You also became imitators of us and the Lord, having received the word in much tribulation with the joy of the Holy Spirit, so that you became an example to all the believers in Macedonia and in Achaia." (1 Thess. 1:6,7)

The power of the Thessalonian church to impact people far removed from them with such force was directly dependent upon the extent to which they accurately represented everything Paul stood for. Paul stresses that they were imitators of the Lord and of them. To the Corinthians he said, " Follow me as I follow Christ". (1 Cor. 11:1)

"For if you were to have countless tutors in Christ, yet you would not have many fathers, for in Christ Jesus I became your father through the gospel. Therefore I exhort you, be imitators of me. For this reason I have sent to you Timothy, who is my beloved and faithful child in the Lord, and he will remind you of my ways which are in Christ, just as I teach everywhere in every church." (1 Cor. 4:15-17)

"Be imitators of me, just as I also am of Christ." (1 Cor. 11:1) The teknon begins to work in active support becoming a fellow laborer in the kingdom work of his spiritual father in the Lord. This support might express itself in a variety of ways (financially, practically, vision casting, prayer, etc.) At this point the teknon son has embraced the building pattern (church doctrine) of the spiritual father and trans-generational grace is being transferred becoming evident to all.

"But I hope in the Lord Jesus to send Timothy to you shortly so that I also may be encouraged when I learn of your condition. For I have no one else of kindred spirit who will genuinely be concerned for your welfare. For they all seek after their own interests, not those of Christ Jesus. But you know of his proven worth, that he served with me in the furtherance of the gospel like a child (*teknon*) serving his father." (Phil. 2:19-22) The teknon lives in the hope and desire of his inheritance and reception of all the promises of His Father. Through inspiration of the Holy Spirit the son is gaining clarity of their purpose in the house of God and he becomes conscious of the fact that he as a co-heir with Christ cannot be joined to any element of bondage.

"And you brethren, like Isaac, are children (*teknon*) of promise. But as at that time he was born according to the flesh persecuted him who was born according to the Spirit, so it is now also. But what does the scripture say? " Cast out the bondwoman and her son (*uhois*), for the son (*uhios*) of the bondwoman shall not be an heir with the son (*huios*) of the free woman." So then, brethren, we are not children (*teknon*) of a bondwoman, but of the free woman." (Gal. 4:26,31)

Compare these passages:

"But when the fullness of time came, God sent forth His Son, born under the Law, so that He might redeem those who were under the Law, that we might receive the adoption as sons (*uihothesia*). Because you are sons (*huios*), God has sent forth the Spirit of His Son (*huios*) into our hearts, crying, "Abba! Father" (Gal. 4: 4-6).

"For all who are being led by the Spirit of God, these are sons (*huios*) of God. For you have not received a spirit of slavery leading to fear again, but you have received a spirit of adoption as sons (*uihothesia*) by which we cry out, "Abba! Father" (Romans 8:14,15).

"The Spirit Himself testifies with our spirit that we are children (*teknon*) of God, and if children (*teknon*), heirs also, heirs of God and fellow heirs with Christ, if indeed we suffer with Him so that we may also be glorified with Him." (Romans 8: 16,17) The witness of the Spirit within the teknon is that he is a son. The Spirit within the spirit of the teknon, CRIES " Abba Father" and is the spirit the son received – a spirit of adoption AS SONS (uihothesia) – a cry for mature sonship. As a teknon, huios is already present within, waiting to be unveiled so that inheritance can be accessed. The Spirit cries from within us, we too cry for it, and creation also eagerly awaits it.

THE NEANISKOS SON

Greek definition

Strong: "A youth" (under 40)

Thayer: "Young man, youth"

Zodhiates: "Young man in the prime and vigor of manhood up to the age of 40 years."

Neaniskos – Young Man in vigor of manhood.

In this son the word of God is alive and sharp. He has overcome the evil one. This son has keen eyes and can see what others can't. This son learns the spirit is poured out to him and through him. He is ready to claim the victory over the largest obstacles in his life.

(In the natural, this describes someone between17– 40).

The Neaniskos sons exhibit a robust and consistent spiritual strength. By having the Word dwelling in them in an abiding and consistent way, they demonstrate a capacity to overcome the world and the enemy. These sons have the grace of God the Father firmly within enabling them to be a model for others. They demonstrate a discerning spirit and cherish the Spirit's presence and leadership in their lives.

"I have written to you fathers, because you know Him who has been from the beginning. I have written to you young men (neaniskos) because you are strong and the word of God abides in you, and you have overcome the evil one." (1John 2:14) He has developed keen vision through persistent use of the word, for the Spirit has been poured out on him and flows through him. The insights of truths concerning God's word are recognized as present-day revelation for a continued building of God's kingdom. By way of the Holy Spirit, this son constantly reviews the words of Christ for understanding Jesus' transformation into the 'Beloved Son of God'. He considers the demonstrative authority displayed in Christ Jesus as the ultimate in representing the Father in the earth.

"And it shall be in the last days, God says, "that I will pour forth of My Spirit on all mankind; and your sons (uihos) and your daughters shall prophesy. And your young men (neaniskos) shall see visions. And your old men shall dream dreams." (Acts 2:17) Note- this verse does not imply that only at the neaniskos or huios stage of development is the Spirit poured out on him. The baptism of the Spirit could take place simultaneously at the initial point of salvation or one's entry into the kingdom of God (e.g. Acts 8:12-17, 10:44,45; 19:1-6)

Here the different stages of development are highlighted to draw reference to the fact that certain abilities associated with the outpouring of the Spirit will be more notable in their formation or maturation within certain stages of sonship development. In the huios son, prophetic capacity will be notably mature and in the neaniskos son, the seeing of spiritual visions (heavenly perspectives) will be prevalent. Vision here could also refer to spiritual sight or perception – to see more clearly and accurately.

The son is positioned to claim victory over the largest obstacles to maturing in his life. These areas are usually what the Holy Spirit has revealed as opportunities for going deeper into the commitment reflected in Jesus' call to "come, follow Me ."

"The young man (neaniskos) said to Him, "All these things I have kept, what am I still lacking?" Jesus said to him, "If you wish to be complete, go and sell your possessions and give to the poor, and you will have treasure in heaven; and come follow Me." (Matthew 19:20) In context, Jesus indicated to the rich young ruler that he should keep the commandments to access eternal life and He lists five of the Ten Commandments when asked to elaborate exactly what commandments to observe. The young man claimed to have kept them all. It is notable that Jesus only lists five commandments that bear reference to how we should relate to others, but leaves the lasts of the Ten Commandments, viz., not to covet. Jesus tested his obedience in asking him to give up all that he has, sell it, transfer the proceeds to the poor and follow Him, if he desires to be mature. (Matt. 19:21) He failed the test, leaving with a grieved heart for he owned much property. Covetousness, greed and a withholding spirit was this young man's problem. Being 'young', he laid great confidence in these things to secure his future. His heart was in his treasure and not in the Lord. Note, the first four commandments relate specifically to one's devotion and love for God. Even if he kept five of the commandments, they were not born out of a singular devotion and love for God. To this young man Jesus laid an expectation to give up all he had, to overcome the pressing desire to self-preserve and self-protect, and obey to a degree where nothing binds him or inhibits him in his desire to follow the Lord. Every neaniskos must cross this phase in their journey towards maturity. Because he is able to see the obvious favor of God through the accumulation of material comfort and the realization of heart desires, he is able to make sacrifices and is willing to lay down all because his heart is set on eternal treasure that will not fade away.

"But store up for yourselves treasures in heaven, where neither moths nor rust destroys, and where thieves do not break in or steal; for where your treasure is, there will be your heart also." (Matt. 6:20) Often this test for the neaniskos son will be reflected in his revelation of sacrifical financial giving as he starts to demonstrate that the spirit of mammon has no hold on him and thus he is eligible to begin to steward riches of the kingdom in Christ. This son has received the truth concerning God's access of resources knowing that true sons are stewards and executive administrators of kingdom provisions.

"He who is faithful in a very little thing is faithful also in much; and he who is unrighteous in a very little thing is unrighteous also in much. So, if you have not been faithful in the use of unrighteous wealth, who will entrust the true riches to you? And if you have not been faithful in the use of that which is another's, who will give you that which is your own?" No servant can serve two masters; for either he will hate the one and love the other, or else he will be devoted to one and despise the other. You cannot serve God and wealth." (Luke 16: 10-13) The neaniskos son recognizes valid apostolic ministry and is able to serve in establishing the son's mandate practically and spiritually. How this son responds to proceeding doctrine impacts their ability to cooperatively become a vessel for bringing other individuals into desiring maturity and sonship.

"And immediately she fell at his feet and breathed her last, and the young men came in and found her dead, and they carried her out and buried her beside her husband." (Acts 5:10) This is not the ordinary deaconship function. The young men representing neaniskos sons walk along side the apostolic function of adhering to the purity of doctrinal truth. The Apostolic seeks to bring the church back to an authentic form and function. To do so, it will extract from the church any false dimension. In Acts chapter 5, Annanias and Saphira had been judged for lies and hypocrisy before the Apostles and the Holy Spirit. At this time in the early church, the apostolic dimension was establishing purity, transparency, righteousness, honor, etc. Young men (neaniskos) came alongside this apostolic function to practically remove that false dynamic which was made void by the apostolic ministry. The neaniskos son starts to appreciate, participate and actively support the apostolic dimension in this regard. This son expunges the false, dead or decayed elements that might impede the forward advance of the Body of Christ, embracing an apostolic mentality and outlook maturing within him.

THE HUIOS SON

Greek Definintion

Strongs: "A son"

Zodhiates: "Huios refers to a legal heir and thus by implication, an adult"

Thayer: "Those who in character and life resemble God, those governed by the Spirit of God, repose calm and joyful trust in God."

Huios – The fully matured son.

When God declared Jesus as His son, Jesus was no longer being seen as the son of Joseph and Mary. "…And behold, a voice out of the heavens said, "This is My beloved Son, in whom I am well pleased." (Matthew 3:17)

God acknowledged Jesus' obedient life as being fully capable of representing Him in every aspect of the Godhead. Huios sons have the fullness of Christ in them as exact representations of Christ reflecting the Father. Christ as a huios of God shared all the graces resident in the Father. Everything He inherited as God's Son is subject to His body, the church. Inherent to all sons of God is pointing individuals back to God as their Father in heaven. As Jesus began to function in His ministry He found Himself fulfilling that mandate of pointing people to the heavenly Father. When He began to call disciples to Himself, He demonstrated His authority to transfer the spiritual inheritances of the Father to His preordained sons. As the Son, Jesus showed disciples how they could be used of God to bring forth "mega-sons", extra large fish capable of feeding many. Jesus demonstrated this ability two times. The first, He directed disciples who were fisherman to cast their nets for a large catch. The second time He directed the disciples He commanded them specifically where to cast their nets and they retrieved a specific number of large fish. The imagery of fish is firstly a catch of souls and secondly a catch of mature souls capable of feeding or becoming an extended source of provision. (Luke 5: 1-11, John 21: 3-14)

Huios sons are fishers of men, individuals who have become workmen participants of the five-fold ministry. The journey for them has been a process of experiencing levels of intimacy with the Father that has increased their faith to know the Father will care for them in every situation, as they trust the voice of the Father. (Matthew 6: 31-33) These experiences are what they share with their spiritual wards entrusted to their care by their spiritual fathers. Huios are able to teach by experience the love and faithfulness of the Father by His word as He considers all sons "firstborn" to Him. He seeks true oneness in maturity with other sons, and does not shrink from God's process of sharpening amidst discipline as He perfects his walk. He is ready to take hold of his full inheritance because in the natural this describes someone of 40 or more. Jesus however, was identified as a huios by the Father at 30 years old. The Huios son demonstrates with consistency submission and obedience to his spiritual father even as the circumstances of life bring sufferings, the huios is able to embrace them as opportunities for shaping their life. (Hebrews 2:10, 5:8) In this season of trials the son is acutely aware of the challenge of compliancy towards God's design for his life. The son yields to the configuration process in word and deed, knowing he's being moved towards the express image of Christ in God the Father. "Beloved, do not be surprised at the fiery ordeal among you which comes upon you for your testing, as though some strange thing were happening to you; but to the degree that you share the sufferings of Christ, keep on rejoicing so that also at the revelation of His glory you may rejoice with exultation." (1 Peter 4: 12,13)

"For I reckon that the sufferings of this present time are not worthy to be compared with the glory which shall be revealed in us." (Romans 8:18)

Jesus was commended and validated by His Father at His baptism because He exhibited total subjection and obedience to Joseph and Mary as His spiritual parents. Thus the Heavenly Father recognized Him as His divine Son. The principle of spiritual fathering is powerfully demonstrated in the book of Ruth, who being the representation of a spiritual son (Ruth 4:15) consistently obeyed Naomi (spiritual father) and came into intimate relationship with Boaz (Christ).

" It is for discipline that you endure; God deals with you as with sons; for what son is there whom his father does not discipline? But if you are without discipline, of which all have become partakers, then you are illegitimate children and not sons. Furthermore, we had earthly fathers to discipline us, and we respected them; shall we not much rather be subject to the Father of spirits and live? For they disciplined us for a short time as seemed best to them, but He disciplines us for our good, so that we may share His holiness. All discipline for the moment seems not to be joyful, but sorrowful; yet to those who have been trained by it, afterwards it yields the peaceful fruit of righteousness." (Hebrews 12: 7-11)

The huios knows that to be illegitimate is more than refusing discipline, which is typical of a nepios rather it is to be marked as misbegotten or "nothos", a false son. This mature son knows the instruction and discipline of the Father through an earthly spiritual father, understanding that such is for their maturation.

"And behold, a voice out of the heavens said, "This is My beloved Son, in whom I am well pleased." (Matthew 3:17) The huios son is confirmed for ministry by His Father to be His Son. Hearing the voice of the Father through a trained listening ear developed over a Holy Spirit led wilderness journey, the huios steps forward into the work of the Father' business of gathering sons unto Himself. The son has learned the business of his father, which is to bring forth other mature sons and is eligible to administrate the affairs of his Father's estate. This son has received affirmative words of encouragement from his spiritual father and responded positively by developing his grace gifting to the body. This son also has evidence of fruit attributable to the grace ministry he has devoted himself to in establishing the kingdom of God. The huios son understands discerningly, he is a part of the greater inherited corporate Son of God.

Jesus was Joseph and Mary's paidon son (Luke 2:40) and their teknon son (Luke 2:45), but was declared by God, the Father, to be His huios son (Luke 3:22). The goal of spiritual fathering is to mature a son in his relationship with God as His Father. The spiritual father although he is always vital, needful, relevant, present and active in relationship, subtly recedes into the background as Joseph did from being the predominant and foremost fathering dynamic in the life of the son. Being the son to an earthly spiritual father is meant to mature you in your relationship with God, your Heavenly Father. If you have a spiritual father, but do not know God as your Heavenly Father, you are still an orphan. Naomi's (spiritual father) goal was to lead Ruth (spiritual son, Ruth 4:15) into intimacy with Boaz (Christ). Ruth's intimacy with Christ produced an offspring (Obed) who produced Jesse, who fathered David, from whose earthly lineage Christ would come (Ruth 4:17). The relationship between God the Father and the spiritual son produces what is needed to change the earth; the return of God's Son as the rightful ruler in the earth and over creation. He will honor and obey his earthly spiritual father, but is focused on the ultimate objective of what this relationship is designed to bring him into, viz., the full formation of Christ within him. The deepening of intimacy with his Heavenly Father and an unswerving expression of obedience to His Heavenly Father marks the life of huios sons. Obedience to God's word is to be led of the Holy Spirit. (Romans 8: 14) Any efforts of the huios, is done strictly through what they see or perceive the Father doing. (John 5: 30, 5: 19-20, 10: 37-38) Communicating truth becomes important towards further equipping the body for the works of God. As the huios speaks, it is with a focused spirit-led mindset, desiring to speak, as God would have him do so. (John 12: 49-50) This son, through the message, seeks to reach the orphaned mind with the love of God while bringing those in growth even closer. He seeks to give to the Father, sons delivered from an orphan's mindset bringing them into sonship. He inclines to seeing the best for others and helping them find the love of the Father through faith and obedience. The huios has become a peacemaker as a Son of God (Matthew 5:9) and is committed to showing the love of God even to those the world has rejected. This son embraces the responsibility to reflect divine love not expecting love in return. The huios understands in his own experience that God loved him first therefore his goal is to replicate this position as a Son to the world. (1 John 4: 10,19)

THE HUIOS SON

One God and <u>Father</u> of all **who is <u>over al</u>l** and **<u>through all</u>** and **<u>in all</u>**. (Ephesians 4:6)

Every thought, word and action in the sons of God must exhibit the nature and will of their Heavenly Father. The huios son will have an intensely intimate relationship with God as His Father and is convinced that God will take care of him always. Its in knowing God as his Father, the huios son has total reliance, dependence and trust in God his Father, and is completely convinced that God will supply all his needs in this life. In his speech, thinking and behavior he demonstrates this mentality and does not contradict it. The following scriptures should be read, rehearsed, reviewed and re-sounded thoroughly: (Matthew 6: 31-33, Hebrews 1:5, Jer. 31:9b, Ps. 89: 26,27)

The huios son knows how to love 'FIRST' in a context in which he himself is not loved. In this way he models the nature of his Heavenly Father (1 John 4: 10,19). It is interesting that the Son, who as an expression of His divine love, forgave sins against him and is called the Son of the MOST HIGH. The phrase 'MOST HIGH' stresses the lofty and superior nature of God. Many times the huios son is described as a son of light, son of the day, son of peace, the son of consolation, or son of resurrection. Each term describes a unique quality associated with this mature son. Sons of the Most High could allude to the fact that a mature son who perfects relationships exceling in love and forgiveness has reached a noteworthy 'height' and 'ascendency'. In his sonship expression the nature and characteristic attributed to God, becomes that of the son Most High. The son quickly forgives men of their sins against him knowing no man after the flesh seeing the seed grace of the Father's love and is now eligible on behalf of His Heavenly Father to administer the forgiveness of sins generally, thus facilitating the entry of men into the kingdom of God.

"If you forgive the sins of any, their sins have been forgiven them; If you retain the sins of any, they have been retained." (John 20: 23)

Huios' sons are often described in various ways to highlight certain characteristics associated with maturity, examples: They are Sons of **the Kingdom** (Matt. 13:30) – not 'son of the house' or just 'son of some spiritual father'. The huios son, while he is the 'son of a man' exhibits behaviors, thinking and levels of commitment beyond his local house and spiritual father to incorporate the wider 'Kingdom'. Kingdom and sonship are inextricably linked – Col. 1:13

Son of **Peace** (Luke 10:6)

Son of the **Day** (1 Thess. 5:5) – i.e. enlightened with true knowledge

 Sons of Light (John 12: 36) – who discloses the nature of God, the Light to men (Matt. 11: 27)

Sons of the **Resurrection** (Luke 20:36) meaning 'partaker of the resurrection'. Hence the principle of LIFE pulsates within the son who 'has LIFE within himself (John 5:26). This son, akin to the last Adam, is a **'life-giving spirit'**, not a 'life-giving soul' like the first man Adam. (1 Cor. 15: 45) This son gives life to men. (John 5:21)

Sons of the **Highest** (Most High) – (Luke 6: 35-36)

The huios son activates his FIRSTBORN status, privilege and function.

"For those whom He foreknew, **He also predestined to become conformed to the image of His Son**, so that He would be **the Firstborn** among many brethren." (Romans 8: 29) Ultimately our conformity to the image of THE SON is conformity to His state as a 'huios' son. This huios son is poised to access all the executive privileges and divine functions attendant with his inheritance in and of God as the FIRSTBORN IN CHRIST. Hence it is critically imperative that sons of God mature toward the huios dimension of sonship as quickly as possible. It is not conditional upon time, but upon willing and obedient co-operation with the demands of the Lord. This is our destination and must always be kept at the forefront of our thinking. For this level of sonship, all of creation eagerly awaits. So do we.

"For the anxious longing of the creation waits eagerly for the **revealing of the sons of God.**" (Romans 8:19)

"The degree to which you walk in the 'measure' of the 'SON' is the degree to which you are able to command and influence the environment around you". As we mature in the fullness of the Son, which is in essence already present within us, we shall be able to righteously express the rule of our Father over all creation. Nothing shall be impossible to us. Jesus commanded creation many times whenever His Father's will deemed it necessary. Creation will respond and subject itself to the mature image of God within His sons.

THE PATER

'Pater' is the Greek word translated in English as 'FATHER'. The level of 'Pater' – FATHER – is possible to the huios son, who has the capacity to accurately represent His Heavenly Father well. It is every huios son's responsibility, privilege and honor to do so. The name of the 'Son' is 'Everlasting Father' (Isa. 9:6,7) – so in sonship the nature (name) and function of father can be expressed. Every mature Son of God must accurately model and put the nature of his Heavenly Father on display for men to observe. So in this sense, 'fatherhood' as seen in the light of a mature son showcasing his Father's character and will in the earth, could be perceived as the highest level of sonship. In essence, the huios son actually does this! Apart from this, also, there are some called to function as spiritual fathers who are given custody of God's sons who may be in various stages of their development (either nepios, paidon, teknon, neaniskos or huios). This individual is to bring the grace of the Heavenly Father to these maturing sons and aid their development to maturity. This is a serious role and function for the one called to it and must be done soberly, sincerely and in the fear of God. These individuals should know the Heavenly Father intimately and deeply, and be acquainted with His ancient and eternal ways.

"I am writing to you, **<u>fathers,</u>** because you **<u>know Him</u>** who has been **from the beginning**..." (1 John 2: 13a)

"...just as you know how we were **<u>exhorting and encouraging and imploring</u>** each one of you as **a father would his own children**, so that you would **walk in a manner worthy of the God** who calls you into His own kingdom and glory." (1 Thess. 2:11,12)

CONCLUSION

Need for maturity

Therefore leaving the discussion of the elementary principles of Christ, let us go on to perfection, not laying again the foundation of repentance from dead works and of faith toward God, of the doctrine of baptisms, or laying on of hands, of resurrection of the dead, and of eternal judgment. And this we will do if God permits.

(Hebrews 6:1-3)

This hope we have as an anchor of the soul, both sure and steadfast and which enters the Presence behind the veil, where the forerunner has entered for us, even Jesus, having become High Priest forever according to the order of Melchizedek.

(Hebrews 6:19-20)

CONCLUSION

For the earth which drinks in the rain that often comes upon it, and bears herbs useful for those by whom it is cultivated, receives blessing from God…Hebrews 6:7

"For the earth yields crops itself: first the blade, then the head, after that the full grain in the head." (Mark 4:28)

God has given birth to sons through His firstborn who is the Christ, born of the Virgin Mary. The impregnation of Mary by God's seed brought about the divine conception placing deity into a human body to manifest a new race.

"For Unto us a Child is born, unto us a Son is given…" (Isaiah 9:6)

The birth of Christ, as a child, was purposed by God. God allowed His son to be affected by every human developmental experience: environmental, social, cultural, and physical. The principle of family is demonstrated and experienced through the relationship of God as Father to His offspring. Jesus was the seed of God becoming the Christ, the Son of God.

As a child, Jesus had to learn of his heritage in the law and the prophets. In birth Jesus was positioned as a son but in obedience he was transitioned into Sonship.

CONCLUSION

Every believer today is positioned through the born again step as a Son of God. Like Jesus, we must experience the sovereignly implanted seed of God by faith into our spirits. That seed of God is the promise of an inheritance as sons of God, the Father. In the seed of God, is everything needed to become matured sons capable of manifesting the complete full image of God, the Father. The process of growth speaks to the principle of rebirth and resurrection in becoming matured, having the ability to reproduce the nature or characteristics of one's progenitor. Even though an individual can be born into a family, they are not immediately capable of the family's influence or abilities.

Through faith the believer is given the power to become a child of God. It is this faith applied in obedience that enables the growth of God's nature and character within. Jesus grew up in a hostile environment. His divinity was not recognized nor was he given special privileges. He had to discipline his mind into what the recorded word declared he was. The prophecies written that spoke of a Messiah to be born had to be received by Jesus as he gave himself to the study of the word. The pursuit of his destiny and developing his relationship with his heavenly Father gave rise to his becoming the true Son of God, the matured Christ. "So the child grew and became strong in spirit…" (Luke 1:80)

CONCLUSION

As Jesus developed his spirit, he became more in tuned to his relationship with his heavenly father. Jesus began to recognize his oneness with the Holy Spirit of his Father, and this revealed to him his pre-existent position as the word of his Father.

Relating to the Father God

Source…as the begotten of God, the church represents God's expression of family as it was meant to be. It is through Jesus Christ the church has been birthed as a family of sons having one God and Father. The church's existence is for the manifestation of the life and kingdom rule of God in the earth. (1 Cor. 8: 6)

Father…the standing of the church in the world must be seen as a separate and called out people. The rulership of God's kingdom in the earth can only be evident as the world's systems are impacted by the church. It's an uncompromising corporate church that will be received as sons and daughters of God. (2 Cor. 6: 16-18)

Unified…the church family has been admonished to communicate in one effort and voice, the glory and praise of God as the Father of the Lord Jesus Christ. Because the church was birthed through the sacrifice of Jesus' finished work on the

CONCLUSION

cross, every part of the believer's life must reflect the provision, purpose and presence of the righteousness of the kingdom of God.

Purpose...it is only as the church relates to God according to His established principle of a father son wineskin that the church's purpose can be fulfilled. Paul said that it was only for that reason, (grasping the plan of God) that he would bow his knees before the Father. The will of God has been placed over, in and through the church with Jesus as the head or elder son. Sons are not only a physical extension of their father but they also represent the graced potential of the Father. The church families of the kingdom derive their name from the Father of heaven and earth, the ultimate and first father. (Eph. 3:14, 4:6)